ISABELLA
AND THE MAGIC UMBRELLA

WRITTEN BY
KATE MAHONEY-VEITCH

ILLUSTRATED BY
SARAH-LEIGH WILLS

For my children: you are my world and my inspiration.
I hope you always make me laugh every day.

Jack, my firstborn, you are kind, thoughtful, funny and silly.
I hope you always have football fever. Forever my little monkey boy.

Isabella, you are my chatty, funny, independent, imaginative,
cuddly little lady. My truly unique Issy Pops.

Vinnie, my baby, you have a mischievous mind and the
cutest smile. Always ready with a kiss and a cuddle.
My cheeky little Vinnie Veitch!

I love you to the moon and back!

ISABELLA AND THE MAGIC UMBRELLA

Illustration and design by Sarah-Leigh Wills.
www.happydesigner.co.uk

Isabella is a little girl who loves soft toys; she has so many of them that they take up most of her bed, the window sills in her bedroom, on top of her wardrobe and bookshelves. She loves them all, but her favourites are Monkey Snuggles, Snuggly Rabbit, Jessie the Cat, Daddy Leopard, Baby Leopard and Duke the Pup.

Isabella also absolutely loves books, she has lots of them; three bookshelves full in fact! She loves looking at the pictures and telling magical stories to her soft toys.

Today it is raining. Mummy is walking Jack
to school with Isabella and their little brother
Vinnie. They all have their wellies on and their
umbrellas up. Isabella jumps in a big puddle:
SPLASH! Oh no, Monkey Snuggles gets all wet!

Isabella is very upset. Her Mummy gives her a hug and tells her not to worry, they will dry him when they get home. Isabella doesn't want Mummy to put Monkey in the tumble dryer so they decide he can dry on the radiator.

When they get home Isabella pops Monkey on the radiator, gathers up her soft toys and starts telling them a magical story.

"One day Isabella and her best friends are getting ready to have a tea party in the garden when it starts to rain. Isabella runs inside to get an umbrella before they all get wet."

"How very strange," Isabella says to her friends. She decides to try once more, but as soon as she closes the umbrella it starts to rain."

"So Isabella and her friends sit and have their tea party under the big umbrella without any rain."

"When they look up at the sky they see a great big rainbow full of red, green, blue, orange, yellow, pink and purple colours."

"Isabella and her friends look up at the rainbow
and then smile at each other and all
agree that it must be a magic umbrella."

"Monkey Snuggles is dry" says Mummy. Isabella gathers up her soft toys, follows her Mummy in to the lounge and they all have a great big cuddle on the sofa.

THE ISABELLA SERIES...

Isabella is a little girl who adores soft toys and books. She loves making up magical stories where her soft toys come to life and have exciting adventures with her.

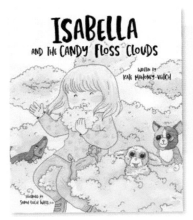

ISABELLA AND THE CANDY FLOSS CLOUDS

In this story Isabella and her soft toys wake up in clouds made of candy floss and discover a sticky world of shapes.

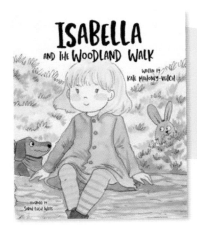

ISABELLA AND THE WOODLAND WALK

In this story Isabella goes for a woodland walk with her soft toys but one of them gets lost!

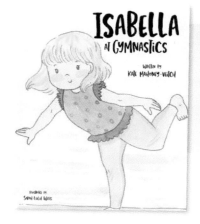

ISABELLA AT GYMNASTICS

In this story Isabella and her soft toys all go to gymnastics and turn a bit wild!

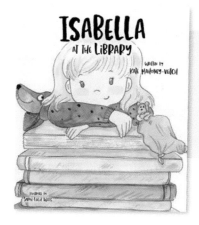

ISABELLA AT THE LIBRARY

In this story Isabella and her soft toys go to the library where they visit the world of nursery rhymes.

ISABELLA AND THE MAGIC UMBRELLA

In this story Isabella and her soft toys discover that they have a magic umbrella.

Printed in Poland
by Amazon Fulfillment
Poland Sp. z o.o., Wrocław